WIPE-CLEAN LEARNING

My First
123

AUTUMN
PUBLISHING

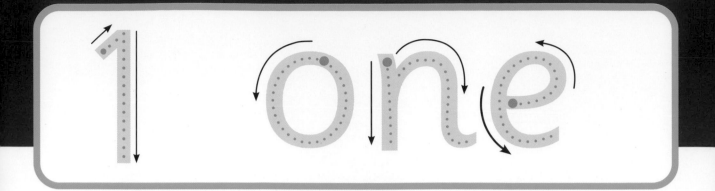

Circle the balloon that is shaped like a 1.

Now try tracing these:

1   1   1   1   1

Teddy is 1 year old. Trace 1 apple in the tree.
What other things can you count 1 of in the picture?

Now try tracing these:

one one one

How many wheels are on a bicycle?

How many wings does a bird have?

How many eyes does the monster have?

Now try tracing these:

Two of something is called a pair.
Trace the pairs of the objects below.

Now try tracing these:

two two two

3 three

Trace the lines to see which race car gets each trophy.

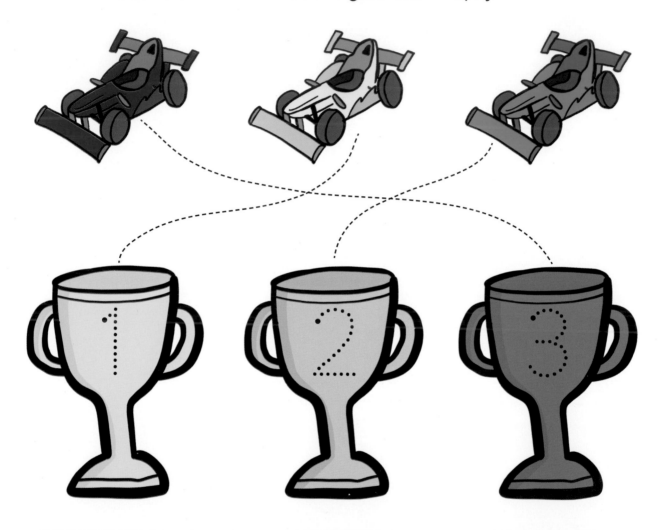

Now try tracing these:

3 3 3 3 3

Trace the numbers on the cars so they're ready to start the next race.

Now try tracing these:

three three

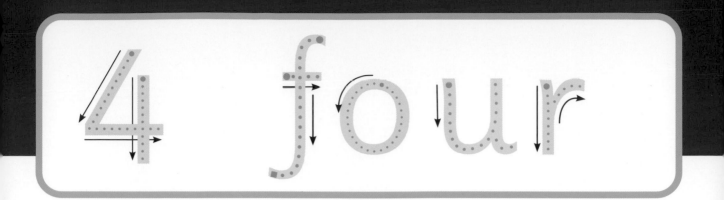

Help the monsters clean up the playground. Find 4 plastic bottles, then draw lines to the bin to recycle them.

Now try tracing these:

4 4 4 4 4

Trace the lines to finish drawing the monsters.

I have 4 arms.

I have 4 teeth.

I have 4 legs.

Now try tracing these:

four four

5 five

Help Hilda Horse eat all the hay. Find a path through the maze, tracing the numbers as you find each hay bale.

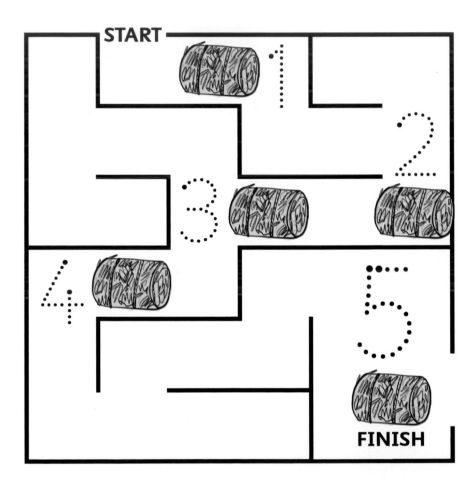

Now try tracing these:

5 5 5 5 5

Mother Hen has lost her chicks. Find and circle them. How many chicks are there?

Now try tracing these:

five five

6 six

Find and circle 6 differences between the pictures.

Now try tracing these:

Now try tracing these:

six   six   six

7 seven

Help Beatrice Bee visit all the flowers. Draw lines to connect the flowers in order from 1 to 7.

Now try tracing these:

7 7 7 7 7

Trace 1 more bee.

How many bees are there now?

Now try tracing these:

seven seven

8 eight

Trace 8 legs on this spider.

Now try tracing these:

Count the flies.
How many are there?

8

Now try tracing these:

eight eight

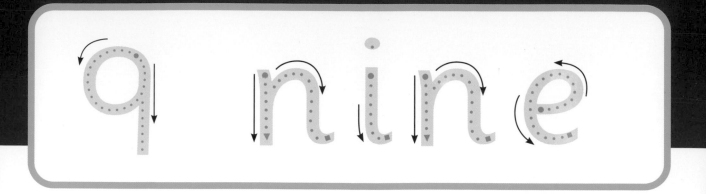

Draw more apples on the trees so they all have the same number.

How many apples does each tree have?

9

Now try tracing these:

9 9 9 9 9

Circle the tree that is different from the others.

Now try tracing these:

nine nine nine

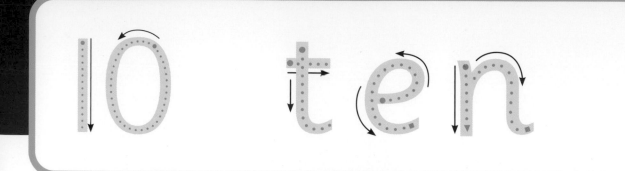

Connect the dots in order from 1 to 10 to finish drawing the robot.

Now try tracing these:

10 10 10 10 10

Can you find and circle 10 aliens?

Now try tracing these:

ten ten ten

Dinosaur sorting

Look at all these dinosaurs! Now answer the
questions. Write the answers in the boxes.

How many dinosaurs have spots?

How many dinosaurs are there altogether?

How many dinosaurs are green?

Draw 10 more teeth on this T. rex.

Circle the dinosaur that
has more spikes.

Are there more red dinosaurs or yellow
dinosaurs? Tick the box by your answer.

Number doors

Can you draw lines to match the letters to the correct doors?

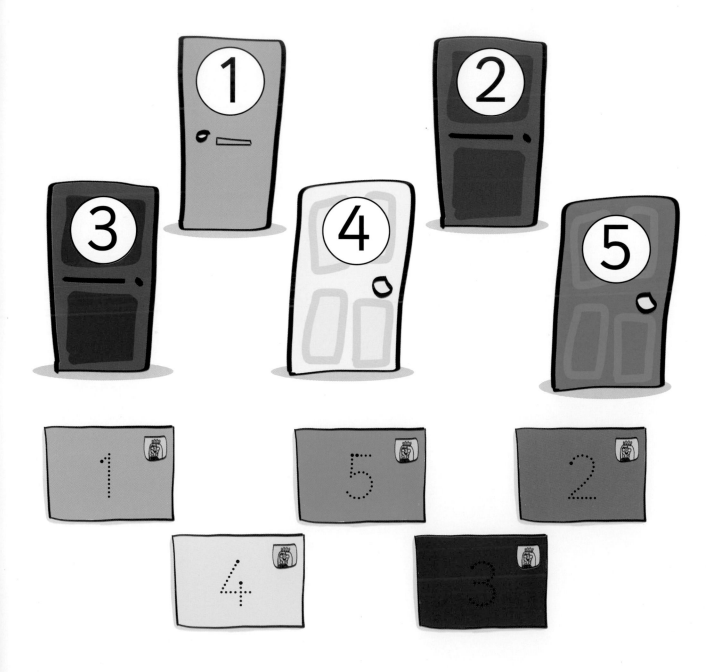

Which number house is each vehicle visiting?
Write the numbers in the boxes.

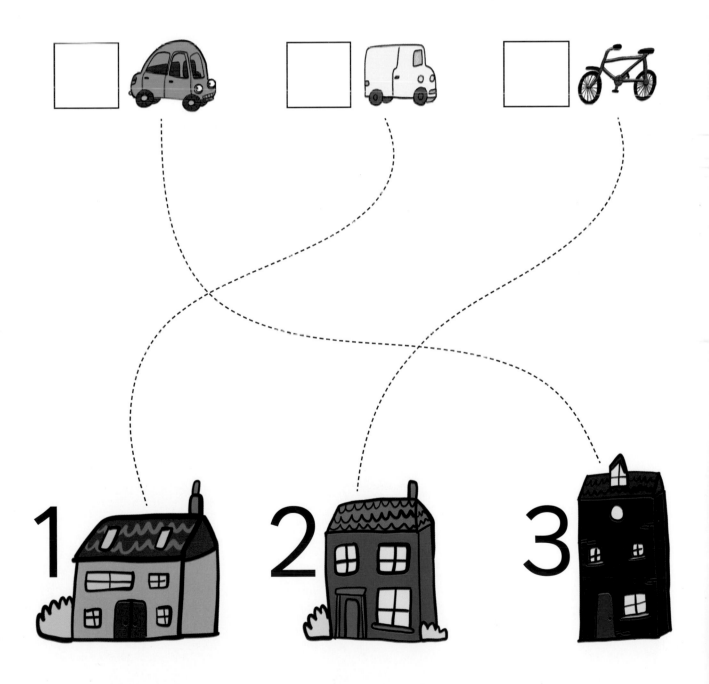

Number burglar

How many crowns does the burglar steal?
Trace the number.

3 crowns

How many spare helmets does the knight have?
Trace the number.

5 helmets

How many rings does the queen have?
Trace the number.

6 rings

Treasure castle

Help the knight find the castle, picking up all the treasure on the way.

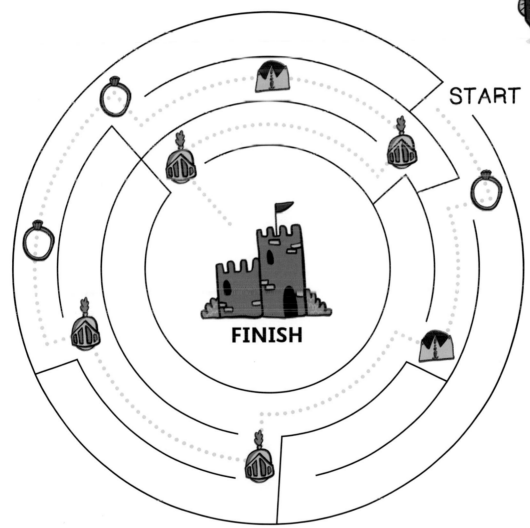

START

FINISH

How many crowns
did you find?

2

How many rings
did you find?

3

Toy shop

Trace the lines to match the toys to the coins that can pay for them.

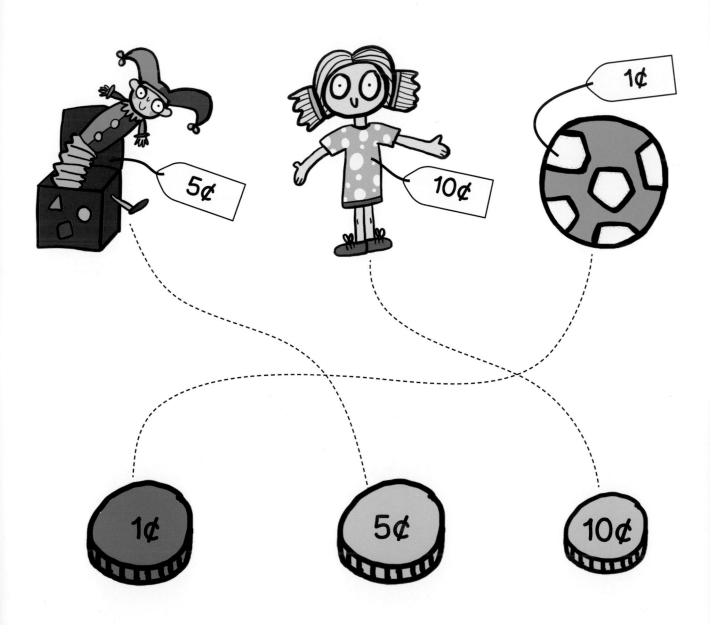

Connect the dots from 1 to
10 to finish the teddy bear.

Teddy has 3
buttons on his
tummy. How many
more buttons
can you find?

5

Spots and stripes

How many spots do these animals have?
Draw lines to match the animals to the numbers.

Draw **7** stripes on the zebra.

Trace the numbers, then draw that many stripes on each bee.

Monkey soccer

Trace the numbers on the monkeys' soccer uniforms. Then trace the line to help them pass the ball in order from 1 to 5.

Trace the numbers to show the scores at the end of each match.

Party pup

It's Pup's birthday! Connect the dots in order to find out how old he is.

1

2

3

4

5

6

7

Trace the candles on the cake so Pup has
the right number for his birthday.

How many candles are there?

7

Robot shapes

Trace the shapes. Then trace the number that shows
how many sides each shape has.

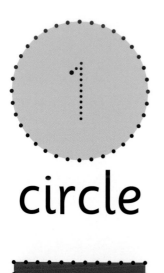
circle

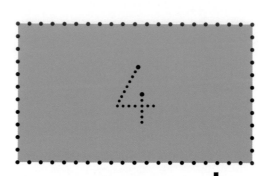
rectangle

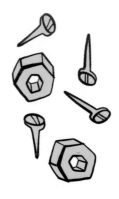

square

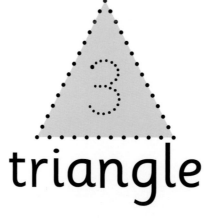
triangle

Now try tracing these:

Try drawing some shapes on
your own in the frame below.

Now try tracing these:

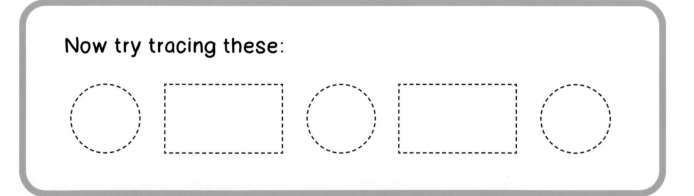

Pirate map

Follow the instructions to help the pirate find the treasure.

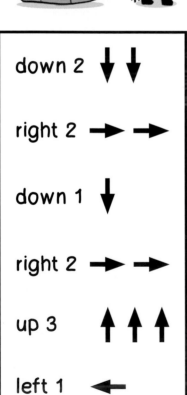

START				

down 2 ↓ ↓

right 2 → →

down 1 ↓

right 2 → →

up 3 ↑ ↑ ↑

left 1 ←

click!
click!

Can you spot the things below in the picture?

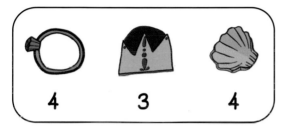

4   3   4

Kitten count

Count these cats' kittens and
write the number of kittens in the box.
Circle the cat with the most kittens.

Kitten colors

Trace the yarn trails to see which color yarn each
kitten has. Circle the correct color.

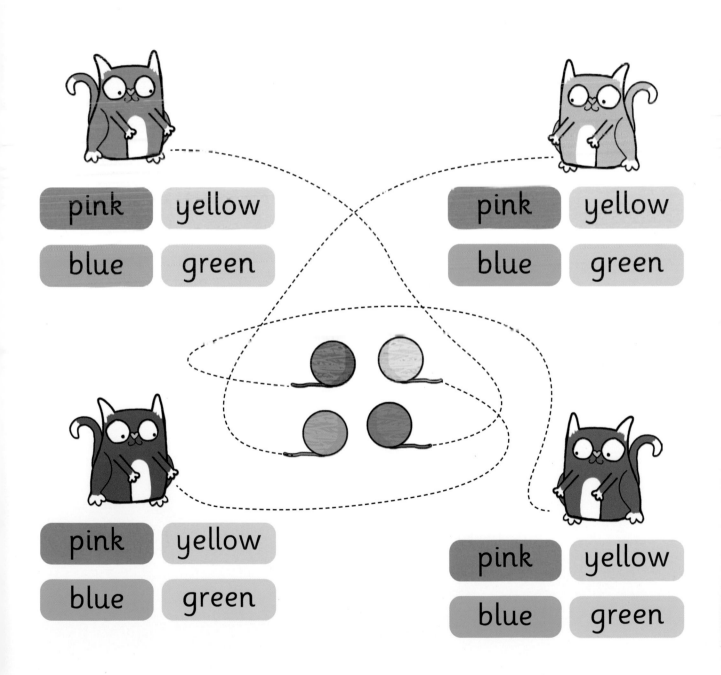

pink   yellow

blue   green

pink   yellow

blue   green

pink   yellow

blue   green

pink   yellow

blue   green

Fruit salad

Trace the numbers to find out how many of each fruit the fruit salad recipe needs. Then draw the correct number of each fruit on the plate.

Fruit salad recipe

Number juggle

Trace the apples to help
Clive learn to juggle.

How many apples
can you see?

5

Numbers 1 to 10

Trace the numbers from 1 to 10.

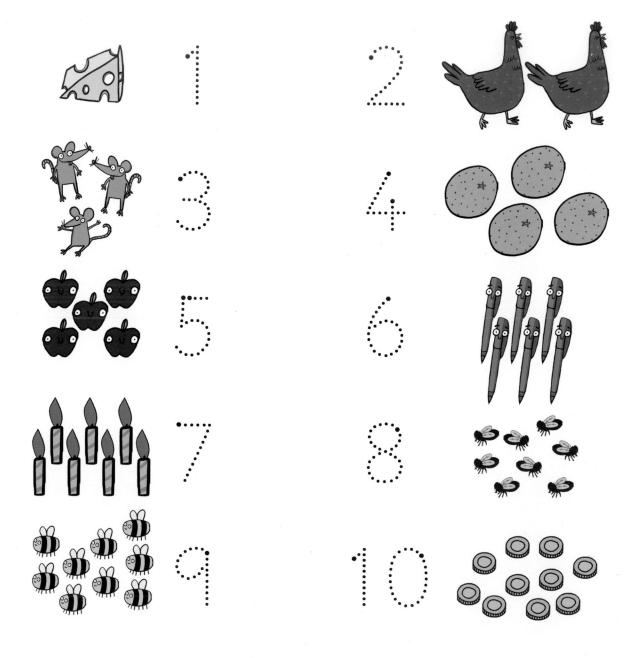

Numbers 11 to 20

Now try tracing numbers 11 to 20.

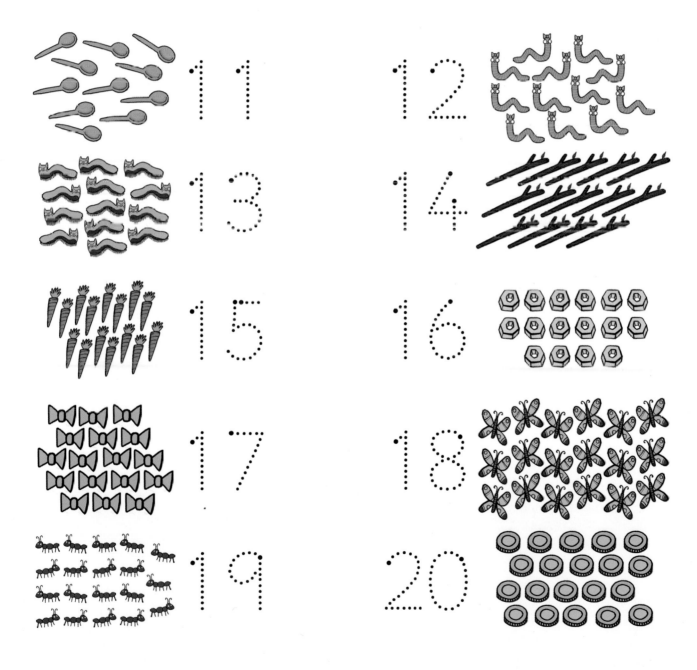

WIPE-CLEAN LEARNING

Give your child a head start at school with this big book of games and activities, reviewed by educational experts. Then wipe the pages clean, and play all over again!

AUTUMN
PUBLISHING

autumnpublishing.co.uk

First published in the UK by Autumn Publishing
An imprint of Igloo Books Ltd
Cottage Farm, NN6 0BJ, UK
Owned by Bonnier Books
Sveavägen 56, Stockholm, Sweden
All rights reserved, including the right of
reproduction in whole or in part in any form.
Educational consultant: Carrie Lewis
Illustrated by Katie Abey
Designed by Jamie Abraham
Edited by Katie Taylor
Manufactured in China. 0423 001
10 9 8 7 6 5 4 3 2 1

US $8.99
CAN $11.99

Climate Neutral
Product

3+

Conforms to ASTM D4236

 WARNING:
CHOKING HAZARD – Small parts.
Not for children under 3 yrs.

ISBN 978-1-83852-785-3

50899

9 781838 527853